HOW TO FIND TRUE HAPPINESS WITHIN YOU

Effective Way Of Making Yourself Happy

ANA M. PHILIPS

Table Of Contents

Chapter 1

Be Kind To Yourself

Life can be difficult since there are so many factors that are out of our control. The avalanche of feelings that appear during trying situations is tough to control. But there are things we can do that will make us kinder to ourselves, especially when we start to feel powerless or hopeless. These challenging feelings have less of an impact on our overall emotional well-being when we are more compassionate with ourselves.

What Does It Mean to Treat Yourself Kindly?

There are four characteristics of self-care:

Talking to oneself with kindness
realizing that everyone experiences suffering
observing your feelings with clarity and objectivity, without stifling or exaggerating them

establishing reasonable expectations for yourself in any given situation

It can be challenging to visualize what treating yourself kindly even looks like if you tend to be self-critical or gloomy. The practice may feel forced, awkward, and artificial. But being kind to oneself might be made easier by recalling how it feels to be kind to others.

Why it's vital to be kind to oneself

Self-compassion and the idea of developing a growth mindset go hand in hand.
You're more likely to forgive yourself as you learn and develop to be your greatest self if you can treat yourself with care and empathy. With forgiveness comes the need to steer clear of making the same errors again.

You have to be kind to yourself to see yourself as a friend.

17 Ways to Be Kind to Yourself

Below you'll discover 17 ways to be kind to yourself.

1. Carve Out Some Time For Yourself.

Every day carve out some time for yourself and do something that brings you joy. You can draw, journal, write short stories, play a musical instrument, or do anything else that you love to do. Be kind to yourself by giving yourself some "me time" each day.

2. Give Yourself Recognition.

17 Ways to Treat Yourself Kindly

There are 17 ways to treat oneself kindly in the list below.

1. Schedule some time just for you.

Make time for yourself each day, and engage in enjoyable activities. You can do anything you enjoy doing, such as sketch, write in a journal, create short tales, play an instrument, etc. Give yourself some "me time" every day to show yourself some compassion.

2. Express Your Own Appreciation.

Frequently, we're quick to applaud the accomplishments of others but reluctant to applaud our own. That must end. Recognize your accomplishments and become aware of them.

When you do anything for which you are proud, take a moment to reflect on it. Self-congratulate and enjoy the accomplishment.

3. Develop Your Inner Activist.

The inner critic is something we've all experienced. It's the inner voice that constantly has criticism to offer and is quick to judge. It's time for your inner critic and inner ally to meet.

Who is this inner advocate, exactly? It's the voice that defends you in your thoughts, another voice. Your inner advocate steps in and makes reasons in support of you when your inner critic mocks and scorns you. Your inner critic is working against you, while your inner supporter is on your side.

Develop your inner ally and be kind to yourself.

4. Be Kind to Yourself.

We are all fallible. Consider what follows:

Perhaps you engaged in behavior in the past that you regret.

Perhaps you failed to stand up for yourself and you let someone else get the better of you.
You may have missed a great opportunity because you got scared.
Maybe you failed to follow through on an important goal.

If you're angry at yourself, you need to show yourself kindness: stop blaming yourself, resolve to do better from now on, and forgive yourself.

5. Take Good Care of Yourself.

One of the best ways to show yourself kindness is to take good care of yourself. Get enough sleep, eat fruits and vegetables, and get some form of exercise regularly. In addition, choose a way to release stress, be well-groomed, and look after your appearance.

5. Look after yourself well.

Taking care of yourself is one of the nicest acts of kindness you can perform for yourself. Get enough rest, consume fruits and vegetables, and engage in regular exercise. Additionally, find a way to decompress, maintain good grooming, and care for your appearance.

6. Honor Yourself

Respecting oneself is appreciating oneself for who one is and refusing to let other people determine your worth.
It involves believing in your abilities to think independently, generate views, and make decisions for yourself. It also involves not comparing yourself to others.

Finally, maintaining your word to yourself and carrying out your plans are key components of having self-respect. Be compassionate to yourself by holding high regard for yourself.

7. Indulge Yourself.

I'm not pushing shopping treatment or industrialism. Nonetheless, assuming you see something that you truly need, indulge yourself. Assuming that it's costly, set something aside for it. You don't need to sit tight for another person to give it to you as a gift. Give it to yourself.

8. Calm Yourself.

Did you have an extreme day? Did you get into contention with a collaborator or a companion? Did you bomb your show? Was it one of those days in which all that could be wrong, did turn out badly? Be thoughtful to yourself by calming yourself. Do the accompanying:

Absorb a hot tub.
Add scented shower oil.
Give yourself a scalp knead.

Rub your feet.

Make yourself some hot chocolate with little marshmallows in it and sit back with a secret book.

Lock your room entryway, turn on some music, and dance around in your clothing.

All things considered, no one knows how to relieve you better than you.

9. Help Yourself to remember you are Great Characteristics.

Perhaps you're somewhat heavier than "the ideal body type", however, you have long, glossy hair.

Perhaps you're not perfect at sports, but rather you're a math expert. Perhaps you tend to be sensational, yet you have an incredible comical inclination.

Continuously help yourself to remember you are great characteristics.

10. Lift Yourself.

At the point when you fizzle, commit an error, or accomplish something wrong, you have two options. You can destroy yourself, or you can lift yourself. Individuals who are benevolent to themselves pick the last option.

Let yourself know being OK is going. Give yourself confidence help by helping yourself to remember your previous triumphs. Then, at that point, concoct an arrangement for managing what occurred, and make a move.

11. Tell Yourself, "I'm Sufficient".

We've all had times in our lives when we've thought, "I'm not adequately attractive, or sufficiently brilliant, or sufficiently able to get what I need." Stop it with the "I'm adequately not" self-talk and supplant it with the accompanying;

"I'm sufficient, similarly as I'm."
"I'm commendable."
"I should be cheerful."
"I have the right to have all that I need."
Furthermore, let yourself know that nothing needs to end up making you commendable. You are as of now enough.

12. Honor Your Fantasies.

Individuals who regard themselves-individuals who are caring for themselves-honor are their fantasies. That is, they don't make light of their fantasies by naming them as senseless dreams. All things considered, they incredibly view their fantasies by transforming those fantasies into objectives and making an arrangement for accomplishing those objectives.

13. Figure out the Perfect balance Among Acknowledgment and Endeavoring.

Part of being kind to yourself is recognizing your true capacity. As was expressed in the past point, you ought to understand what you need and pursue it.

Notwithstanding, never being happy with where you are, or with what you have accomplished such long ways throughout everyday life, is being unpleasant to yourself.

Be thoughtful to yourself by figuring out the perfect balance between being content with what your identity is and making a move to turn out to be far superior.

14. Quit Attempting to Be Awesome.

Individuals who set a norm of flawlessness for themselves are getting themselves into a position of disappointment.

All things considered, flawlessness is impossible. Might you at any point consider much else cruel than making achievement incomprehensible for yourself?

Rather than setting a norm of "flawlessness" as far as you might be concerned, means improving, with extra care.

15. Show Yourself Sympathy.

In the book, How to Be Your Own Closest companion by "Mildred Newman and Bernard Berkowitz", the writers suggest that you get to know yourself by showing yourself sympathy. The most ideal way to feel empathy for yourself is to envision that somebody you love is feeling hurt. Check the accompanying out:

What might you tell them?
How might you treat them?
How might you console them?
How might you cause them to feel focused on and cherished?

Presently, do that for yourself — show yourself empathy.

16. Put stock In Yourself.

Part of being kind to yourself is needing awesome for yourself. Furthermore, to get the best, you want to trust in yourself.

Have confidence in your capacities and your judgment. Respect yourself: put stock in yourself.

17. Acknowledge Yourself.

Acknowledge yourself as you are. You have qualities, and you have shortcomings. In some cases, you succeed, and here and there you fizzle. In some cases you're correct, and here and there you're off-base. Permit yourself to completely be what your identity is.

End

There's just a single individual on the planet you'll constantly have a relationship with, and that is yourself.

Subsequently, you better begin ensuring that you're a decent ally to yourself.

Carry on with your best life by being benevolent to yourself. You can begin with the 17 hints that made sense of the above.

Chapter 2

Defining Limits

Recollect social examinations or geology classes in grade school. Your instructor presumably showed you a guide and made sense of that particular sorts of lines were utilized to show limits among states and nations.

Of the time there would be a characteristic component (frequently a waterway) that would separate one area from another, yet generally, the lines we see on the guide were not apparent, all things considered. But, although we can't see the limits, individuals acknowledge that they're there and comprehend how far they can go before crossing into another area.

For different reasons, this idea is a lot more straightforward to get a handle on a guide than it is concerning our connections. More often than not, (sadly) there aren't strict, actual obstructions among ourselves and others. What's more, in any event, when there are, these limits don't necessarily in all cases work, and you can observe that others are going too far somehow or another.

This is where setting allegorical (or even strict) individual and profound limits become possibly the most important factor.

They're your approach to telling others how far they can go with you with regards to things like daily reassurance and work, looking for your assistance or exhortation, or even how as often as possible you're supposed to reach out.

Be that as it may, for the present discussion about private and profound limits, as a general rule, they can be indistinct to distinguish and, surprisingly, trickier to set.

Certainly, we realize we should "put down stopping points," yet what precisely does that mean, and how precisely do we do that? Not at all like geology, this isn't something we scholarly in school.

The majority of us were never prepared how to make it happen and cultivate solid connections in our own lives. To assist you with getting a superior comprehension of individual and profound limits, including how to set them and stick to them, here's some (requested) guidance from prepared experts.

Setting Limits

Individuals discuss "defining limits" constantly, however, what does that mean? "Limits are the partitions that people need — intellectually, inwardly, and truly — to have a solid sense of security, esteemed, and regarded," says Carla Marie Masculine, Ph.D., a clinical clinician in Sonoma District, Calif. also, creator of Bliss From Dread and Date Shrewd.

It implies expressing what influences your solace levels.
At last, limits address what we distinguish as making us agreeable or awkward, says Leela R. Magavi, MD, a specialist and the territorial clinical head of Local area Psychiatry and MindPath Care Focuses. What's more, this frequently includes utilizing verbal systems.

"People could utilize brief, clear expressions to address and explain their solace level and needs," she proceeds.
"For instance, [during COVID] an individual could deferentially request that friends and family wear their veils, stand further away from them and one another, or clean up. This training at home might facilitate any inconvenience while talking with neighbors and individuals from the local area."

It implies figuring out how and when to say "no."

Another vital — yet troublesome — part of defining limits includes figuring out how to say "no" to other people. "Ordinarily we feel that we owe others a paper-level reaction to why we can't do this undertaking, go to this occasion, and so on," says Melissa Rock, PsyD, an ensured clinical injury supplier and academic partner of clinical brain research at Midwestern College in Arizona.

.

"The truth is, a decent limit is a clarification all by itself. 'Please accept my apologies, yet I can't focus on dealing with that undertaking throughout the end of the week. I value you considering me and believing in me, yet not this time!' is a sufficient reaction."

It's Likely Time for a Profound Self Registration — This is The way to Make it happen
It implies telling the truth and straightforwardly.

Yet, going with a cognizant choice to define specific limits isn't sufficient: You should likewise impart those limits to individuals they include. "Defining limits likewise incorporate telling others they — not anticipating that others should have a precious stone ball and simply understand what you need or don't need," Rock says.

It implies knowing how to extend — or choke — the limits we set.

It's likewise important that an individual with solid limits can change their limits relying upon the circumstance to masculine consider the suitable degree of association, says. "By and by, we intentionally and unwittingly use limits to tell others OK or suitable," she makes sense of.

"At the point when our limits are excessively penetrable, we could generally allow individuals to exploit us, or acknowledge harmful treatment. At the point when our limits are excessively unbending, we could act in profoundly shielded ways to keep conscious, cherishing individuals a good way off."

Why Limits are Significant

Considering that limits assist us with feeling more secure and more agreeable, it's a good idea that they come up so regularly in treatment: They can significantly affect our psychological prosperity.

"Our close-to-home limits are significant because they give us the individual space — profound, mental, physical, etc. — we want in a given circumstance," Masculine makes sense.

"At the point when our close-to-home limits are regarded, we feel esteemed, respected, and safe. Limits can be mending; limits can help one not feel exploited." And keeping in mind that keeping up with limits can be troublesome, it increments self-empathy and confidence by permitting individuals to focus on their voice and needs, which Dr. Magavi makes sense of.

The Genuine (and Exceptionally Ordinary) Reason You're So Depleted After Treatment

In any case, when our profound limits aren't regarded, it might leave us feeling overpowered or tormented, or restless.

That, yet assuming our limits are persistently disregarded, the continuous sensations of sadness and frailty can set off constant tension, despondency, and even injury," Masculine says. "On an instinctual level, we might feel like confined creatures who are helpless before compromising culprits when our limits are affronted."

Also, limits are imperative, Masculine says since they make the establishment of sound associations with oneself and with others. "At the point when solid limits are absent, individuals can be passed on feeling furious or miserable because of cooperations that make a feeling of being exploited, depreciated, overlooked, or harassed," she makes sense of.

Normal Signs Limits Are Required

Limit issues emerge in a wide range of circumstances and different pieces of our life, yet it's typical for them to go unnoticed until they've been tested, Masculine makes sense.

"As a rule, limit issues will quite often happen from permitting your limits to be crossed, or crossing others' limits," she notes.

As indicated by Masculine, a couple of the most widely recognized signs that your limits need consideration include:

Feeling persistently exploited in specific circumstances, for example, inwardly, monetarily, or actually.

Saying "OK" to satisfy others on your own.

Not getting your requirements met because you will more often than not dread clash and yield to other people
Frequently feeling disregarded by others, yet not defending yourself.

Apprehension about being dismissed or deserted leaves you tolerating less than you merit.

Participating in human satisfying ways of behaving to be preferred and to get the endorsement.

Taking part in a discourteous way of behaving that harms others.

Playing with the people who are seeing someone as well as a tease when you are seeing someone when it hurts others.

Doing anything you desire to get your requirements met — accepting that cutoff points don't concern you.

However, remember that defining limits might be more enthusiastically for certain individuals than others.

As per Dr. Magavi, individuals who live with uneasiness or potential sadness might battle with making and keeping up with limits. "A few people get solace from how others see them and may stay away from limits to satisfy others," she makes sense of. "Notwithstanding, this could prompt burnout and inactive animosity."

limits to satisfy others," she makes sense of. "Notwithstanding, this could prompt burnout and inactive hostility.

The most effective method to Define Limits (the Correct Way)

Since you have a firmer handle on what limits are and for what reason they're so significant for keeping up with our emotional well-being, you might be considering how, precisely, to define the limits you want in your life. Here are a few systems and models from our specialists to assist you with getting everything rolling.

Thoroughly consider what you want/need to achieve by defining limits.

You may not quickly realize what parts of your life most needing limits, and that is Not a problem. Give yourself the existence for mindfulness, and reflection, and then deal with your viewpoints and gain a feeling of clearness. This should be possible by talking through them with a specialist or cherished one, or thinking of them down in a diary, Dr. Magavi says.

"Expressing and naming feelings permits people to comprehend alternate points of view and causes a solicitation to show up more like a solicitation instead of an analysis," she makes sense of.

Utilize your qualities as an aide.

With regards to defining limits, Rock says they should be by your qualities. "On the off chance that I profoundly esteem my time for strict articulation, my limit might be to never acknowledge a work shift during administration times," she makes sense of.

"When I do, the area being pushed aside is one I value highly, and I feel even more encroached upon." She notes that we do have some control over scenarios like these when we are mindful of what our values are, and prioritize what brings us contentment, fulfillment, and joy.

Comprehend that various connections require various limits.

Limits are in many cases altogether different relying upon the circumstance and individuals required, as per Masculine. For instance, you might have truly adaptable limits with a private accomplice. "Closeness flourishes when the two accomplices get it and honor each other's limit needs, and this deferential demeanor adds to the continuous limit adaptability," she makes sense of.

In a work setting, notwithstanding, it is fitting for managers and staff individuals to have more unbending limits. "Certain ways of behaving, like sharing of individual data, sexual contact, and being a tease —, particularly among the board and staff — are by and large unseemly, and frequently unlawful," Masculine notes.

Furthermore, concerning relatives, the idea of sound limits relies upon general relational peculiarities. "On the off chance that relatives will generally be tyrannical, genuinely inflexible limits might be required for mental prosperity," she says. "If relatives are conscious and accommodating, limits might be undeniably more adaptable in nature."

Assess your connections.

Realizing that various kinds of connections require their arrangement of limits, now is the right time to investigate those connections. "For you to know where you want to set up limits, you want to assess your connections and what you esteem in your life," Rock says.

"On the off chance that you're not getting enough of what you esteem — like family time, monetary security, and so forth — then how would you define a limit to help the satisfaction of bringing my life into more adjust? Limits are much of the time experimentation as we start. It is alright to 'change' them over the long run with the goal that they are the right articulation of your cutoff points."

Understand that it takes practice and tolerance.

For certain individuals, in any event, pondering defining limits can set off tension. "As you work on defining limits, you may feel restless and disrupted until it becomes regular," Masculine makes sense. "Regardless of whether it's intense right away, work on expressing your reality with pride, mental fortitude, and regard."

Make some noise (consciously).

When you begin to sort out what parts of your life could profit from limits, begin making strides toward executing them.

As indicated by Dr. Magavi, this could include things like asking somebody for lucidity, consciously amending somebody, or communicating distress with somebody's way of behaving.

Be that as it may, don't be shocked on the off chance that your issues with an individual don't vanish after tending to them once. "It very well might be important to emphasize data," Dr. Magavi says. "Setting an establishment and permitting liquid discussion toward the start or any place of a relationship hardens an example and permits solid limits to stand tall and solid.

On the off chance that people don't regard limits, it is fitting to fight that this causes distress and leave the relationship."

Focus on relationship changes, and hold your ground.

At the point when you lay out solid limits, normally, individuals who are utilized to you being a mat might get bothered or disturbed. Masculine says that some might try and keep on disregarding your limits.

"As you push ahead, you'll find that certain individuals will be strong of your sound new limits," she notes. "Others might be reluctant to acknowledge and respect the 'upgraded you.' Now and again the most astute move is to limit any association with the individuals who decide not to regard your limits.

Chapter 3

Your Internal Exchange

Additionally alluded to as "inner exchange," "the voice inside your head," or an "inward voice," your inside speech is the consequence of specific cerebrum systems that make you "hear" yourself talk in your mind without really talking and framing sounds.

Your 'inward discourse' is just your contemplations. The little voice in your mind remarks on your life, whether that is what is happening around you, or what you are thinking deliberately or sub-deliberately.

We all have an inward exchange, and it runs constantly. A few of us, notwithstanding, may focus harder on it than others, and be more gifted at controlling it. It is how you apply rationale to what's going on, albeit the rationale may now and again be slanted or driven by your feelings or encounters.

The Significance of Interior Exchange

Interior exchange is important for what makes us human, and especially empowers us to reason and contemplate circumstances.

In any case, what you think, and the language you use can influence your mindset, fearlessness, and confidence. This is the premise of Neuro-Etymological Programming.

Your interior exchange can in this manner be both useful and pointless. For instance:

On the off chance that you are leaned to be restless, your inner exchange can support this. A few observers recommend that

tension can likewise furious your inside discourse, making an endless loop;
Similarly, as grinning encourages you, being presented with negative language and miserable considerations can affect your state of mind. This remembers for your interior discourse if it tends towards 'thumping yourself';

Having the option to have a good inner exchange, and 'look on the splendid side', can assist you with feeling more good and working on your temperament.

This consolidates to recommend that figuring out how to deal with your interior discourse is probably going to be significant for both mental prosperity and possibly, progress throughout everyday life.

Dealing with Your Inward Discourse

1. Becoming Mindful of Your Inward Discourse

Before you can deal with your interior discourse, you first need to turn out to be more mindful of it.

A few of us are exceptionally mindful of our inner exchange, as a consistent presence in the cerebrum, or even a continuous discussion. Others are significantly less in this way and may find it harder to tune in. One method for becoming mindful of it is to have a go at doing some contemplation since this assists you with focusing on your viewpoints.

One more procedure prescribed by certain individuals is to deliberately think 'I can't help thinking about what my next thought will be. Whether this upsets your inner exchange, or simply occupies your mind, it appears to give a space for the cerebrum to become mindful of what is working out.

What you are predominantly attempting to become mindful of is the kinds of contemplations you tend towards, including:

Where your inside discourse goes if you let it meander.

This can provide you with a smart thought of what is irritating you at some random time;
Whether you will quite often think emphatically or adversely;

Your prevailing time direction (past, present, or future); and
Your inspiration (whether you will generally ponder needing all the more beneficial things or less terrible ones, or whether you invest energy attempting to comprehend how things connect).

2. Changing Your Inner Exchange

Whenever you have become more mindful of what you are thinking, and the sorts of examples that your considerations will generally make, you can then take care of evolving them, if essential.

There are a few significant manners by which you can help yourself.

Think Emphatically, not Adversely

It is not difficult to fall into the snare of 'thrashing yourself' inside and condemning yourself constantly. Searching for ways of improving is great, however, accusing yourself since you have neglected to accomplish isn't. It means quite a bit to attempt to stay away from negative reasoning in your inner exchange.

One method for doing this is to deliberately change what you are thinking. If you 'hear' yourself thinking something negative, center around something positive all things considered. For instance, rather than contemplating what you fouled up, ponder what you will do another way sometime later, what you have realized, or even what you got along with admirably.

A Practice Backward Reasoning

On the off chance that you battle to keep away from negative reasoning, attempt this activity:

Next time you wind up thinking something negative, deliberately ponder the inverse, however considerably more so (say, twofold, or much more). Consider it in a lot of detail: how it would look and feel, how it would cause you to act, etc.
Notice how this affects you.

Attempt to Embrace the here and now

Your interior exchange frequently will in general zero in on the past ('What could have been) and the future ('What may be). Zeroing in on the present thusly both quietens your inward exchange a bit, and assists you with focusing on, and appreciating, what's going on at this point.

Be Thankful for What You Have

One method for redirecting your contemplations, and especially to keep yourself from needing pretty much is to ponder what you must be thankful for. This assists you with being more certain because you are searching for positive qualities in your day-to-day existence.

Halting Pointless Inward Discourse

We as a whole have minutes how our inward discourse appears to go off without anyone else, and can twist into a negative outburst. At the point when you feel this event to you, it very well may be useful to advise yourself to stop, as this pulls you up short, and advises you that this is pointless.

Certain individuals track down that a firm yet delicate mental tone, and emphatic 'Stop that!' works best, and others want to stand up clearly to get the full impact.

You might have to investigate to find the equation that turns out best for you.

Controlling Your Interior Exchange Takes Time and Practice

Like some other mental activity or practice, it requires investment to figure out how to pay attention to, and afterward control, your inside exchange. From the get-go, you will likely think that it is troublesome. The more you practice, notwithstanding, the simpler it will get, even though you will in any case have times when you battle. This is ordinary.

It is, nonetheless, significant not to exacerbate it by pummeling yourself since you have neglected to deal with your viewpoints!

All things being equal, simply credit it to experience, and continue. In the future, it will be more straightforward.

Chapter 4

Controlling Negativity

Negative thinking can contribute to problems such as social anxiety, depression, stress, and low self-esteem. The key to changing your negative thoughts is to understand how you think now (and the problems that result), then use strategies to change these thoughts or make them have less of an effect.

"Our thoughts, emotions, and behaviors are all linked, so our thoughts impact how we feel and act. So, although we all have unhelpful thoughts from time to time, it's important to know what to do when they appear so we don't let them change the course of our day," explains Rachel Goldman, Ph.D., a psychologist and clinical assistant professor at the NYU School of Medicine.

Therapy can often help change negative thoughts, but you can also learn how to change your thought patterns. This book discusses some of the steps you can take to change your negative thoughts.

Practice Mindfulness and Self-Awareness

Mindfulness has its roots in meditation. It is the practice of detaching yourself from your thoughts and emotions and viewing them as an outside observer. Practicing mindfulness can help you become more conscious of your thoughts and build greater self-awareness.

Mindfulness sets out to change your relationship with your thoughts.

1. Try viewing your thoughts and feelings as objects floating past you that you can stop and observe or let pass you by.

Become aware of how your thoughts are impacting your emotions and behaviors. Observe your thoughts. Ask yourself if this thought is helpful. What purpose is the thought serving you? How does the thought make you feel?
— RACHEL GOLDMAN, PHD
The objective of mindfulness is to gain control of your emotional reactions to situations by allowing the thinking part of your brain to take over. It's been theorized that the practice of mindfulness may

facilitate the ability to use thoughts more adaptively.

One study found that people who engaged in a mindfulness practice experienced fewer negative thoughts after exposure to negative imagery, suggesting that mindfulness may lessen the impact of negative thinking.

2. Mindfulness Meditation for Anxiety

Identify Your Negative Thoughts

As you observe your thoughts, work on identifying and labeling cognitive distortions and negativity.

For example, if you tend to view yourself as a complete success or failure in every situation, then you are engaging in "black-and-white" thinking. Other negative thinking patterns include:

Jumping to conclusions: This distortion involves making assumptions about what others are thinking or making negative assumptions about how events will turn out.

Catastrophizing: This pattern of negative thinking is characterized by always assuming that the worst possible outcome will happen without considering more likely and realistic possibilities.

Overgeneralization: This pattern is marked by a tendency to apply what happened in one experience to all future experiences. This can make negative experiences seem unavoidable and contribute to feelings of anxiety.

Labeling: When people negatively label themselves, it affects how they feel about themselves in different contexts. Someone who labels themselves as "bad at math," for example, will often feel negative about activities that involve that skill.

"Should" statements: Thinking marked by "should" statements contribute to a negative perspective by only thinking in terms of what you "ought" to be doing. Such statements are often unrealistic and cause people to feel defeated and pessimistic about their ability to succeed.

Emotional reasoning: This involves assuming that something is true based on your emotional response to it. For example, if you are feeling nervous, emotional reasoning would lead you to conclude that you must be in danger. This can escalate negative feelings and increase anxiety.

Personalization and blame: This thought pattern involves taking things personally, even when they are not personal. It often leads people to blame themselves for things they have no control over.

Unhelpful thinking patterns differ in subtle ways. But they all involve distortions of reality and irrational ways of looking at situations and people.

Goldman suggests that this step is all about identifying and labeling negative thoughts. "Now that you have observed the thought, you can identify it as an unhelpful thought (perhaps we've even identified it as an all-or-nothing thought, or another type of cognitive distortion). Just observe it and label it," she suggests.

She also suggests pausing to accept the thought for what it is. Remind yourself that it's just a thought and not a fact.

Recap

Many different types of cognitive distortions contribute to negative thinking. Learning more about these distortions and remembering that thoughts are not facts may help lessen the power of these negative thinking patterns.

Replace Negative Thoughts

One of the basic parts of a treatment plan involving cognitive behavioral therapy (CBT) is cognitive restructuring. This process helps you to identify and change negative thoughts into more helpful and adaptive responses.

Whether done in therapy or on your own, cognitive restructuring involves a step-by-step process whereby negative thoughts are identified, evaluated for accuracy, and then replaced.

Goldman suggests examining the evidence that either supports or contradicts the thought. Doing this can help you challenge negative thinking and explore alternatives that are more helpful and realistic.

Although it is difficult to think with this new style at first, over time and with practice, positive and rational thoughts will come more naturally. Cognitive restructuring can help you challenge your thoughts by taking you through steps including:

Asking yourself if the thought is realistic.

Think of what happened in the past in similar situations and evaluate if your thoughts are on course with what took place.

Actively challenge the thought and look for alternative explanations.
Think of what you'd gain versus what you'd lose by continuing to believe the thought.
Recognize if your thought is a result of cognitive distortion, such as catastrophizing.
Consider what you'd tell a friend having the same thought.

Johns Hopkins Medicine suggests trying to focus on the positive to help combat the negative thought patterns associated with depression. Ask yourself, is there any good to come out of your current situation?

However, Goldman recommends not replacing negative thoughts with overly positive ones. If the replacement thoughts are not realistic, they won't be helpful.

You don't want to set yourself up for failure by replacing the thought with something that may not be realistic. A helpful technique could be to ask yourself what would you say to a friend in this situation.

— RACHEL GOLDMAN, PHD

Goldman suggests that if you find yourself thinking thoughts like "I am a failure"/"I am going to fail," you shouldn't replace them with something like "I know I am going to succeed."

"You instead would want to replace it with something more neutral, which is also showing some self-compassion, like 'I don't know if I am going to be able to do it, but I am trying my best,'" she suggests.

One study found that a single cognitive restructuring intervention helped people reduce negative thoughts and biases that play a role in contributing to anxiety.

Avoid Thought Stopping

Thought-stopping is the opposite of mindfulness. It is the act of being on the lookout for negative thoughts and insisting that they be eliminated.

The problem with thought-stopping is that the more you try to stop your negative thoughts, the more they will surface. This is known as thought rebounding.

Mindfulness is preferable because it gives less weight to your thoughts and reduces the impact they have on you.

Experts believe that the thought rebounding that takes place after trying to stop negative thoughts is much more damaging.

Instead, psychologists generally recommend finding ways to deal with negative thoughts more directly.

Though stopping might seem to help in the short term, over time, it leads to more anxiety.

Practice Coping With Criticism

In addition to cognitive restructuring, another aspect of CBT that is sometimes helpful for those with social anxiety involves something known as the "assertive defense of the self.

Since it is possible that some of the time, people will be critical and judgmental toward you, you must be able to cope with rejection and criticism.

This process is usually conducted in therapy with a pretend conversation between you and your therapist to build up your assertiveness skills and assertive responses to criticism. These skills are then transferred to the real world through homework assignments.

For example, if faced with criticism in real life, having a set of assertive responses prepared will help you deal with these potentially anxiety-provoking situations. What's more, real-life encounters are welcome as a chance to put into practice this exercise, according to this method.

Some research suggests that facing potential "social mishaps" that contribute to anxiety and negative thinking can also be helpful.8 The goal of improving your ability to handle criticism and rejection is to help increase your tolerance of the distress these things may cause, which may combat your automatic negative thoughts.

Use a Thought Diary

Thought diaries, also called thought records, can be used as part of any process to change negative thinking. Thought diaries help you identify negative thinking styles and gain a better understanding of how your thoughts (and not the situations you are in) cause your emotional reactions.

Most CBT treatment plans will involve the use of a thought diary as part of regular homework assignments.

For example, a thought diary entry might break down the thought process of a person on a date, and the emotional and physical reactions that result from negative thinking patterns. By the end of the thought analysis, you can replace irrational thoughts about rejection with more helpful and positive ways of thinking.

What are negative thoughts?

Negative thought includes negative beliefs you might have about yourself, situations, or others. They can affect your mood and can be present in certain mental health conditions.9 Examples are, "I'll never be good enough," "They must think I'm stupid for saying that," and "That situation is destined to turn out badly."

Why do I have negative thoughts?

Negative thoughts are quite common. You might have negative thoughts because we're more influenced by negative than positive, or have a negativity bias. It's also possible that evolutionarily speaking, negative thinking was more conducive to survival.10 Negative thoughts could occur as a result of cognitive distortions. They can be symptoms of mental health conditions such as depression and anxiety.11

A Word From Verywell

If you struggle with negative thought patterns and it's impacting your life, consider talking to a mental health professional. While it can be tough to share the thoughts you have with someone, therapists can assess your negative thinking patterns and help you create a healthier inner dialogue.

Goldman likes to remind her clients that the process of changing negative thoughts isn't a quick fix. "This isn't easy and it takes time, but with practice, it gets easier and you can create new automatic thoughts that work for you," she explains

Chapter 5

An Aide For Taking Care Of Oneself

Definitive Taking care of oneself Aide

Assuming you've at any point flown on a fly, you've heard the well-being guidelines that are reported over the speakers before the flight. You could recall the piece of the content that says: "in case of an unexpected loss of compartment pressurization, breathing devices will naturally slip from the roof. Snatch the cover, and pull it over your face. Assuming you have kids going with you, secure your veil before helping with theirs."

Those headings generally sounded weird to me until I halted to think about the rationale behind them. Since numerous kids don't have the capacity or mental attention to put a breathing apparatus over their faces, it depends on a grown-up to help their youngsters in that cycle. In any case, on the off chance that a grown-up doesn't attach their veil first, they might drop from dazedness and neglect to help their children.

The standard behind those preflight directions additionally applies to your psychological and actual well-being. Maybe you have individuals — kids, kin, a companion, or even guardians — who rely upon you for everyday help. If you're not dealing with yourself, how might you expect to deal with them?

1. Deal with NUMBER ONE

You've presumably heard the maxim "consistently deal with number one." Albeit that truism probably won't be the best counsel in business, group activities, connections, or numerous different everyday issues, it holds a lot of importance to your well-being.

How you treat your body, and cerebrum might well decide your capacity to work in an undeniably bustling world.

Like it or not, stress is a typical and inescapable piece of living. From work or school to shopping and covering bills, the rundown of requests on our time can appear to be difficult.

Assuming it seems like your feelings of anxiety are being stretched to the edge, you might be encountering the sort of weariness that can prompt serious temperament and rest issues. Dealing with yourself might expect you to search for extra assistance. Fortunately, there are numerous functional advances you can take to get the help you want.

2 . GET SOME Dietary Help

Whether you wind up having negative or genuine concerns, or on the other hand assuming you feel that your feelings of anxiety have almost arrived at the limit,

.Notwithstanding supplements, there are numerous other compelling ways of further developing your profound prosperity to oversee temperament and decrease pressure.

Figure out how to be kinder to yourself by executing the tips in this Taking care of oneself Procedure Guide...

3. GIVE YOURSELF A Break

You might feel strained to be everything to everybody, except there's just such a lot one individual can achieve. Increment your energy and endurance by giving yourself a break. We all need time to re-energize our batteries and taking care of oneself is in many cases everything thing you can manage. Additionally, others will benefit when your pressure is decreased and your temperament is gotten to the next level.

4. Pay attention TO Calming TUNES

Nothing unexpected standing by listening to music can increment pleasurable sentiments, further develop temperament, support energy, raise dopamine levels, and help with concentration and focus. Staying in a casual perspective is more straightforward to achieve when you have a cheerful tune going through your mind. Pay attention to mind-improving music explicitly created to upgrade temperament, appreciation, inspiration, and motivation.

5. GET QUALITY Rest

Great rest is fundamental for the ideal cerebrum and body well-being. Deficient and conflicting rest can build touchiness, irritability, and misguided thinking. To stay in your prime, it's suggested that you get 7-9 hours of rest every evening. Whether you're too wired to even think about resting or too focused to even consider dozing, regular tranquilizers can assist with working on your nature of rest.

6. Record IT On paper

The most common way of journaling gives distressing considerations a home, somewhere else they can reside other than your cerebrum. When those considerations have been communicated, they frequently lose their force and earnestness which will permit you to unwind intellectually. Writing in your diary 10 minutes before you hit the sack can assist with delivering the burdens of the day and put you in a relaxing perspective.

7. GET Normal Activity
The actual activity is maybe the absolute most significant thing you can do to keep your mind solid. Exercise can support the

bloodstream and other positive supplements to the mind, increment your degrees of dopamine and create new synapses that can help the cerebrum self-direct and quiet down. Strolling can assist you with clearing your psyche, declining uneasiness, working on your mindset, and consuming a few calories all simultaneously.

8. Ponder Everyday

Set aside a few minutes for yourself consistently. Enjoying reprieves for contemplation and unwinding give advantages to both your physical and psychological wellness. Spending only 15 minutes alone, without interruptions, may invigorate your brain. Clearing your psyche and easing back your breathing can assist with reestablishing internal quiet. Rehashing basic words like "May I be no problem at all" can increment positive feelings and reduction pessimistic ones. Cherishing Benevolence Contemplations can decrease torment and further develop other psychological wellness challenges.

9. GET A Backrub

One method for countering the impacts of pressure is to get a back rub. Knead treatment has been known to increment dopamine levels by almost 30% while diminishing cortisol (a pressure chemical) levels.

10. Simply SAY NO

Assume command over your timetable instead of allowing it to control you. Express no to desires, occasions, and exercises that aren't fundamental for your life. Be aware of what you do, and how you invest your significant investment. Try not to do things the same way since that is how you've generally done them. On the off chance that what you're doing isn't making you blissful or is causing you stress, now is the ideal time to accomplish something else.

By following these temperament-supporting and stress-decreasing methods they can assist you with being blissful and to further develop your general prosperity so you can deal with yourself and the other notable individuals in your day-to-day existence.